Tears of the forgotten girl

A collection of short poems

~

Mahalingham

Tears of the forgotten girl; a collection of short poems

A CIP catalogue record for this book is available from the British Library

ISBN 978-1-4716-7857-8

May 2012

Tears of the forgotten girl; a collection of short poems

CONTENTS

Introduction   7

Tears of the forgotten girl

I.   The intervention   14

II.   Mortal touch   18

III.   Sealed in the rain   22

IV.   Beauty unrivalled   26

V.   Luminous intensity   30

VI.   The rider ascends   34

VII.   Embraced by a father   38

VIII.   A new champion   42

IX.   A bold advance   46

X.   Force of will   50

XI.   Defiant one   54

XII.   The rider falters   58

XIII.   A final intervention   62

XIV.   The forgotten girl   66

Chronology and location of key events   70

Appendix: Poems by Nita Mahalingham

I.   On the birth of our first child   74

II.   The bond between a parent and a child 78

May 2012

Tears of the forgotten girl; a collection of short poems

CONTENTS (Continued)

About the author   82

End notes   85

Tears of the forgotten girl; a collection of short poems

~

Tears of the forgotten girl; a collection of short poems

For Nita

Tears of the forgotten girl; a collection of short poems

Introduction

Tears of the forgotten girl; a collection of short poems

The forgotten girl, Nita Mahalingham, was born an only child in the UK in September 1975. Her childhood was one of great suffering having lost her mother, Saroj, to aggressive cancer when she was just six years of age (see *The forgotten girl*). Saroj is referred to in the text as "suus angelus": her angel. The tragedy was compounded by Nita being forced to accept a vindictive step-mother who mistreated her with frequent emotional abuse whilst her father looked on with apathy.

The author was involved in a car crash in December 1999 which by all accounts should have killed him. He was driving maniacally at night during a thunderstorm and this is where the poem begins. *The intervention* opens with a "Cimmerian rider", reflecting his dark state of mind at the time, charging to his death. Despite the existence of a stable and loving family environment, the author was in a selfish and self-destructive cycle of excess which led to this crash. The author acknowledges the part his elder brother ("Sage counsel") paid in helping him realise the results that his wasteful death at a young age would have had on the family.

Those close to the author are convinced that something or someone intervened in the car crash to save his life (such was the low probability of walking away from this incident unscathed). Suus angelus is the obvious person to have intervened (recognising that the author could help her daughter and that she could help him).

Irrespective of the metaphysics, surviving the crash dramatically changed the author's approach to life and he met Nita (see *Mortal touch)* a few months later whilst he was taking steps to turn his life around. Since meeting Nita, his professional rise has been meteoric and the author attributes this to her support and his need to provide her with a life that she was denied.

The author draws upon mythological influences in the text to emphasise their story: For example, the Hindu God of destruction, Lord Shiva is symbolised here as "The Bowman" and represents death. Other mythological references include:

Tears of the forgotten girl; a collection of short poems

- "Karnan adherence" – strong and unquestioning adherence inspired by this character from the Mahabharatha[i].

- "Bane of Ksatriya" – this refers to the Hindu sage Parasurama who wiped out generations of warriors from the Ksatriya[ii] caste with an axe.

- "Surya charges with the centaur" – Surya, the Hindu Sun God, charging with the centaur (in this case Sagittarius) denotes late November/December when the sun enters this Zodiac house.

- "Liberation in the Supreme" – This quote is taken from the Bhagavad Gita[iii] and refers to a soul attaining peace in the afterlife.

The constant references to "fortune", "fathom" and "fate" demonstrate the authors belief (or "illusion" – see *Beauty unrivalled*) that luck, reason and destiny have been deflected to some extent in their lives. This central message in the text is represented by the three arrows of the Bowman/Lord Shiva.

The author's father, Maha, was a farmer from the Jaffna peninsula of Sri Lanka who toiled to become a chartered engineer in the United Kingdom. He worked long hours to provide a solid home and a life away from a war-torn paradise for his two sons. There are clear references in the text to "the great teacher" ("great" being a literal translation of Maha in Sanskrit). He is the second intervening angel in the text (see *The final intervention*) having become a significant father figure to Nita (see *Embraced by a father*). Maha was pained by Nita's childhood story (his wife, Siva, had also lost her mother at a young age) and he was thankful that his son that most had written off as a cautionary tale was able to rebuild his life with Nita's assistance.

Tears of the forgotten girl; a collection of short poems

The text spans a 12 year period from the time of the car crash until the birth of the couple's daughter in 2011. There are references in the text to numerous events that many would attribute to co-incidence. For example, the last rites of Nita's mother were performed in a South London location. The names of the author and Nita can be found to this day etched in memorial tablets on the funeral parlour walls facing each other. These "appellations" are Sanskrit in derivation; however, they were carved many years ago in the UK parlour on opposing walls as if the couple's union were prophesised (see *Mortal touch*).

Beauty unrivalled and *Luminous intensity* are framed by breathtaking visions of nature that the couple has encountered together. Free from light pollution, the sheer number of stars witnessed whilst on the Andaman Sea on Christmas Day 2003 seemed impossible giving rise to the assertion that stars (synonymous in the text with souls) "long imploded" must have returned or been reignited for a brief moment. However, these particular poems relate more to Nita and her ability to emerge from her past unscathed and with beauty as opposed to the scenes of nature described. The author, who is intolerant to a fault, still marvels at how his wife has surfaced from her traumatic childhood without anger or bitterness. The author substitutes the term "intervention's reward" in the text as a proxy for Nita's smile and he has also included two poems given to him by Nita over the years in the appendix. These poems show that she feels gratitude for her life rather than regret- it is difficult to read *The bond between a parent and a child* without feeling remorse for Nita's own lack of parental support growing up and recognising her desire to ensure her children will have what she was denied. Nita's poems are written in free verse and make an interesting contrast to the rigid metre applied by the author.

Nita is now a successful Optometrist (the "eyes" referenced in *Mortal touch* relate to their first meeting as patient and consultant). She is adored by her family, friends, colleagues and patients.

Tears of the forgotten girl; a collection of short poems

The couple were married in December 2001 and have three children – Luther King, Reeve and Larisa-Lee (who are themselves, significant sources of inspiration to the author and the subject of poems in the text – See *A new champion, Force of will, Defiant one* and *The final intervention*).

Tears of the forgotten girl; a collection of short poems

~

Tears of the forgotten girl; a collection of short poems

Tears of the forgotten girl – the poems

May 2012

Tears of the forgotten girl; a collection of short poems

I.   The intervention

Tears of the forgotten girl; a collection of short poems

Cimmerian[iv] rider charging through the night,

No people to warn, no purpose to serve,

Consumed by rage born out of injustice,

He hastens to his death.

Dark countenance and life of improvidence,

Exiguous the mourning for his reckoning,

An end foretold by fate, fathom and fortune;

Arrows of the Bowman[v].

Across the chasm the forgotten girl waits,

No champion, no protector; none to aid,

Her moment of self-redemption at hand,

The years of pain now spent.

Startled by a deafening noise, she turns

Toward the terrible events that unfold:

"Pour soul, I have felt the cold grip that awaits..."

Tears fall for the undeserved.

Tears of the forgotten girl; a collection of short poems

Cumulating speed with fierce concentration,

The immortal bow strung, the Bowman takes aim,

Arrows so armed that must now destroy their mark,

But then intervention.

Not of fate nor of fathom nor of fortune:

Suus angelus[vi] searching for reparation,

Ending this night with crushing certainty,

To preserve a lost soul.

Deflected, the arrows target new marks,

Shattering self-loath, ignorance, arrogance,

The rider returns home to rehabilitate,

Sage counsel is heeded.

As he pledges to find and protect the girl,

The Bowman retires with thundering gait,

Yet the unavoidable price shall be paid,

Ever watchful of the rider.

Tears of the forgotten girl; a collection of short poems

~

Tears of the forgotten girl; a collection of short poems

II.   Mortal touch

Tears of the forgotten girl; a collection of short poems

The rider's search concludes in a path of Kings[vii],

Eyes, not a window but a door to his soul,

The faintest touch but he will not leave her side,

Interventions reward.

He offers little to the forgotten girl:

Not wealth, nor riches, nor estate, nor title,

Only great strength and a rose encased in glass,

She accedes to fall in love.

The rider holds true to this pledge of respect:

None shall mistreat her, none shall prejudice her,

For he will cast down any who would essay.

Laughter returns to her.

Carefree and thankful for the rider's advance,

She sees the significance of their joining,

And of arrows deflected by a known force...

They seek out her blessing.

Tears of the forgotten girl; a collection of short poems

Strained journey to hallowed place of memory,

Fraught with resurfacing pain once suppressed.

She must endure to obtain affirmation,

And she looks for a sign.

At first, disheartened by cold isolation,

But an unsettled rider points the way:

Two appellations on opposing walls,

None would believe. None could.

Etched by suus angelus on departure,

The union foretold, credence provided,

A blessing bestowed upon the couple,

Affirmation for the girl.

Duly delivered in the depths of her hurt,

They alone share the secret and the augur.

In years hence, this will stay the rider's unrest,

For their hands have been placed.

Tears of the forgotten girl; a collection of short poems

~

Tears of the forgotten girl; a collection of short poems

III.   Sealed in the rain

Tears of the forgotten girl; a collection of short poems

They commence their journey with expectation,

Fortune ever absent, but they are content.

She inspires a necessity within him,

To rise above the crowd.

He toils to provide for the forgotten girl,

He commits under the weight of affection,

Mobilising courage to blaze a new trail.

The measure of a man.

The girl unaware of the rider's decree,

Never has she braved the notion of this night,

Her story is replete with disappointment:

"How long will he remain?"

But she is satisfied with short lived fervour.

The rider grows impatient with the girl,

Still he makes ready for this night of accent,

Adorned with white armour.

Tears of the forgotten girl; a collection of short poems

A pier extends over the murky waters,

The rider motionless in contemplation,

Waiting to deliver a promise to the girl:

A promise of protection.

Waters that once froze[viii] run true on this night,

And he leads the girl to secure their pact,

An offering carved once in a thousand years,[ix]

Will bind him to his pledge.

The rider knelt down in obeisance,

The forgotten girl rooted in disbelief,

Unaccustomed territory for this dyad,

Raindrops pierce the river.

The rain, an asseveration from above?

The proposal is delivered to silence…

Intervention's reward, lucid memory,

Burned into their vision.

Tears of the forgotten girl; a collection of short poems

~

May 2012

Tears of the forgotten girl; a collection of short poems

IV.   Beauty unrivalled

Tears of the forgotten girl; a collection of short poems

They are surrounded by fortress of ice[x],

Far away from the world they form life's plan,

With time slowed to permit their discourse,

He is captivated.

A resonant crack paves way for the thaw,

The air fresh with new opportunity,

"How could this charge be created in torment?"

He observes her reverie.

Rage now replaced by passionate desire,

To account for traumatic events of yore,

She strays, overcome in a dreamlike state,

In this place of stillness.

They reside together away from the host,

The rider empowered by her solace,

Are they able to control fate, fathom and fortune?

The illusion sufficient.

May 2012

Tears of the forgotten girl; a collection of short poems

Their journey continues to higher ground,

A majestic and noble creature appears,

Searching the rider's eyes for recognition,

The girl takes a step forward.

A gentle but firm warning is delivered,

Trembling, she shelters behind the rider,

But then succumbing to intervention's reward,

They continue on their path.

One cold night they rest beside still waters[xi],

Perfect isolation, no others in sight,

The universe starts to unfold around them,

Stars pierce the indigo.

Alpine ladder stretching to the eternal,

Enhanced with celestial light from above,

The rider captivated only by the girl:

Her beauty exceeds all.

Tears of the forgotten girl; a collection of short poems

~

Tears of the forgotten girl; a collection of short poems

V.   Luminous intensity

Tears of the forgotten girl; a collection of short poems

A journey to the land of their fathers,

Spiritual realisation of his line,

Many years since the first rider's charge,

To serendipity[xii].

Son begets son begets son, tilling the earth,

Subsisting in this tranquillity and peace,

Until one journeyed the length of an empire,

And the Bowman took aim.

The rider and the girl sail upon an ocean,

A place of answered and unanswered dreams,

A mystical lake[xiii] attracts hopefuls to its cause,

But many leave unfulfilled.

An island off an island is their retreat,

Alone with the splendour of this world,

A pallet of purple and gold is displayed,

As the Saviour's day closes.

Tears of the forgotten girl; a collection of short poems

They look up through a perfect hemisphere,

No obstacle within view, nothing breaks the milieu,

Luminous intensity pales the ebony,

Those long imploded return...

Creating a constellation of constellations,

For how else could the multitude be explained?

Humbled by the totality of souls,

Awe-struck by the majesty.

The forgotten girl finds harmony at last,

Stillness and strength craved and now received,

Can they hide here away from the world?

No longer a need to hide.

Intervention's reward lights the path ahead,

She embraces him to ensure he is there,

And they salute those who brought them together.

Sailing home, they shall return.

Tears of the forgotten girl; a collection of short poems

~

Tears of the forgotten girl; a collection of short poems

VI.   The rider ascends

Tears of the forgotten girl; a collection of short poems

He labours, thousands of hours at his craft,

Perfecting his trade as never before,

Day and night, sacrificing all to succeed,

Sacrificing all for her,

To provide no more than the girl deserves,

To become the man that she alone beholds,

Credibility provided to her faith:

He shall prevail for her.

She cares for his needs as he slaves to excel,

Lifting his fatigue with her advocacy,

Aware is she of his potential to be:

The spark she has witnessed.

The spark that will ignite this institution,

Precognition of the rider's resolve,

To be counted among the most worthy,

She presages his triumph.

35

Tears of the forgotten girl; a collection of short poems

Task after task, a relentless tirade,

He does not cease in his pursuit to upgrade,

No allowance for error, in this test,

Principal of principals.

An ordeal not designed for the faint of heart,

His hour has arrived, he must prove his worth,

When called to the arena, the challenge met:

Confirmed by august body.

Cumulating speed once more but controlled,

The rider charges with a staunch purpose,

All others left in his wake, none believe,

He exceeds expectation…

All except that of the forgotten girl,

Her expectation not exceeded but met,

His achievements made through her endorsement.

Ascent of the rider.

Tears of the forgotten girl; a collection of short poems

~

Tears of the forgotten girl; a collection of short poems

VII.   Embraced by a father

Tears of the forgotten girl; a collection of short poems

A lost prince, restored to the succession,

Kinsman welcome the forgotten girl home,

She is honoured and accepted as their own,

And she will be cherished.

One seeks her out from the jubilations,

He above all others knows their saga,

At last, she is embraced by a father,

Allied to the rider.

The rider's great teacher in meditation,

He visualises the past endurances,

Unaware how to repay the rider's debt,

Yet he will find a way.

He observes the young couple with dignity,

And becomes lost in distant memory,

His promise made to a girl long ago,

He recalls their story.

Tears of the forgotten girl; a collection of short poems

The forgotten girl is celebrated,

To redeem a childhood of isolation,

She is a foreigner to this kindness,

The rider vaunts his prize.

Much cause for elation, much cause for joy:

Two lives duly preserved by providence,

By the intervention made in his favour,

They squander not this gift.

This night, a new chapter will begin for them,

Their lives forever extended and enriched,

She turns her head to the rider as before,

But no tears fall this night.

A crescent moon adorns the evening sky,

But no cause for consternation or alarm,

A golden period commenced for this house,

It shall last an aeon.

Tears of the forgotten girl; a collection of short poems

~

Tears of the forgotten girl; a collection of short poems

VIII.   A new champion

Tears of the forgotten girl; a collection of short poems

Vast courage but lingering doubt surfaces:

Has he the worth to foster in the new?

Fortune's absence not rued until this moment,

A path that he has feared.

Certain the past will now shape the future,

Of this undeserved rider in thought,

One night in the abyss of his regret,

She displaces the fear.

An effortless speech duly delivered,

And the emergence of a fearless rider,

No limits, no constraints, no hindrances,

An heir to bring honour.

To seek out and protect the world's beauty,

He will carry the weight of expectation,

Upon shoulders crafted in hard endeavour:

An augmented rider.

43

Tears of the forgotten girl; a collection of short poems

Born under the watchful eyes of great twins[xiv],

His temperament and his calm school the rider,

The boy is cherished by all who draw near,

And peace comes to the girl.

The rider pens a letter to transcend years:

Instructions to protect the girl should he fall,

And she will never again be forgotten,

The rider immortalised.

The new champion is exceptional:

With grace unexpected but still welcomed,

Inherent compassion seldom encountered,

He will alter the world.

The people's army will shape his fortune,

Swearing his fealty to the rider's cause,

Karnan[xv] adherence to his relentless will,

Generations preserved.

Tears of the forgotten girl; a collection of short poems

~

Tears of the forgotten girl; a collection of short poems

IX.   A bold advance

Tears of the forgotten girl; a collection of short poems

A plot of greed forces the rider to halt,

He is rendered without option, without choice,

His instinct to advance but he carries them,

So he puts aside his dream.

A safe road presents itself to the rider,

He reluctantly bows his head in assent,

To see out his days under their command,

To join a lesser clan.

But the forgotten girl speaks with assertion,

She instructs the rider with her grand force:

"You cannot retreat, you must brave forward".

Stunned by this account...

But spurred on by what he knows to be right,

He picks up his sword and takes to the field,

Risking much with single comrade in arms,

To not fight would risk more.

Tears of the forgotten girl; a collection of short poems

Many hours of heavy combat ensue,

And the rider has secured a new empire,

An empire that will not diminish or wane,

Captains of utmost skill.

An opportunity undreamed is seized,

Fortune favours the rider's bold advance,

The girl has aided a forgotten rider,

Blessed with munificence.

The rider takes up his place in history,

She is proud of his endurance and resolve,

And others view the rider through her eyes,

His accolades are hers.

Made possible through her words, her belief,

She retires and tends the new champion,

Untested in battle, yet strong of heart,

He provides that denied.

Tears of the forgotten girl; a collection of short poems

~

Tears of the forgotten girl; a collection of short poems

X.   Force of will

Tears of the forgotten girl; a collection of short poems

The rider bears a terrible burden:

Young progeny slain upon the battlefield,

Outwardly, he does not despair, he is strong,

For the forgotten girl.

Incapable of preventing cursed events,

What use is he to the bane of the ksatriya[xvi]?

He rides on through the forest to begin anew,

Unable to aid the child.

Lamentation for this life that might have been,

Perpetual tears fall for a deserved soul,

"Let my favour pass to this innocent",

The girl begins to weep.

"Protect my child from these tribulations,

Profound potential has he to succeed",

He lays lifeless and she informs the rider...

Her tears not required.

Tears of the forgotten girl; a collection of short poems

The rider consumed with a familiar rage,

"What purpose could be to this shortest of lives?"

The sins of the father on the unoffending:

Guilt racks his moral core.

He takes refuge and imbibes to dull his pain,

Unbeknownst, the young warrior takes control,

To rise from the field and confront assailants,

This is no illusion.

Refusing to be felled by the arrows,

A physician's miracle is his force of will,

His strength is evident to the rider:

He will not acquiesce.

The girl gives thanks to her answered prayer,

The rider charges through the night once more,

To bring them home from this exacting ordeal,

He will be tested again.

Tears of the forgotten girl; a collection of short poems

~

Tears of the forgotten girl; a collection of short poems

XI.   Defiant one

Tears of the forgotten girl; a collection of short poems

His eyes, a semblance of the forgotten girl,

But the rider's consuming rage dwells within,

Forced into combat before he could stand,

But he is not helpless.

In distress, his eyes fix upon the heavens,

Summoning his strength from a distant place,

None but the girl can sooth his pain and sorrow,

As the rider before.

Once again he draws fire from the Bowman,

But he is too young to match this onslaught,

"Visit your evils upon me and me alone"

The rider rages skyward.

The Bowman heeds not the rider's commands,

The debt must be paid, the lesson must be learned,

With nothing to offer the young combatant,

Still, he flails in vain.

Tears of the forgotten girl; a collection of short poems

The fever - unbearable heat none could withstand,

The girl stands alone keeping vigil over him,

She prepares her farewell, "fight no more my child,

I cannot bear your suffering"…

Unassisted, the defiant one battles with success,

He meets the Bowman's volley with his axe[xvii],

Stark annihilation of the arrows,

The girl in exaltation.

His resolve now twice proven on the field,

Will the terrible challenge come again?

Trials to hone his skills, forged in discontent,

Until called to serve,

To defend the land with undaunted power,

The rider fears not for this protector,

For it is in his small hands to control:

Preserved for a purpose.

Tears of the forgotten girl; a collection of short poems

~

Tears of the forgotten girl; a collection of short poems

XII.   The rider falters

Tears of the forgotten girl; a collection of short poems

This day the rider grows weary and falters:

A failing neither of drive nor of skill,

A lack of precision weakens the stronghold,

The stone wall has cracked.

He sees not the forthcoming onslaught,

For he has other preparations to make,

Sorrow for the loss of his great teacher,

Elevated through clouds.

The enemy strikes hard and strikes fast,

He has no answer and yields in neglect,

Yet the girl will become his redemption,

Sacrifice without hesitation.

Her belief in the rider does not wane,

She tends his wounds and quiets his rage,

The chance to strike back is soon at hand,

Assisted from beyond.

Tears of the forgotten girl; a collection of short poems

The rider recoils, regroups and repairs,

Solid groundwork to counter this foe,

Determined that she will not suffer or settle,

He plans the recovery.

With controlled and meticulous execution,

Emerging through insurmountable challenge,

A victory through graft, precision and humility,

A resounding triumph.

A victory through her endorsement once more,

For alone he would surely have fallen,

They move forward and rebuild with caution,

Suring the foundations.

They strengthen the areas of attack,

The uncompromising foes are allayed,

A bright future dawns for the forgotten girl,

He will not falter again.

Tears of the forgotten girl; a collection of short poems

~

Tears of the forgotten girl; a collection of short poems

XIII.   The final intervention

Tears of the forgotten girl; a collection of short poems

They forge iron foundations together,

Plans made in their fortress of ice long ago,

Arrows still dart toward their position,

But they are deflected.

They can survive and outlast any attack,

For he fights with the girl at his side,

The rider reliant on her abetment,

A proven comrade in arms.

There is a final intervention to come:

One that shall set right the initial wrong,

The forgotten girl's void has become a mother's:

A final account settled.

A precious gift can restore the balance,

And give back what she had taken away,

A house of joy ready for benefaction,

The protectors in wait.

Tears of the forgotten girl; a collection of short poems

She arrives when Surya charges with centaur[xviii],

With rays propelled through clouds upon the child,

The great teacher forever present with them,

A debt that is repaid.

Recalling a wayward son saved on that night,

Protected from the Bowman's deadly arrows,

He has long lamented the girl's anguish,

And he removes her pain.

Final intervention for the forgotten girl,

To permeate the void with this blessed life,

He speaks to the young couple with affection:

"Rider, protect the child".

To the forgotten girl – "let the scar heal",

The great teacher 's final commands are heard,

Assured of liberation in the Supreme[xix]...

His soul is now at rest.

Tears of the forgotten girl; a collection of short poems

~

Tears of the forgotten girl; a collection of short poems

XIV. The forgotten girl

Tears of the forgotten girl; a collection of short poems

"Angelum meum being torn away,

Her pain will be scarred upon my pure soul,

Why does she seek to impel me away?"

Unable to face the girl:

"Who will take care of her, who will protect her?"

She retains her beauty throughout the ordeal,

The forgotten girl looks to those who could aid…

They compound her agony.

"I stand an unwanted statue in their lives,

An obstacle to their cold union",

A burden of guilt to the mongrel ménage.

They pray she were not there.

"None come to my aid, save one weary soul,

My partner in suffering, to share this pain,

My self reliance is necessitated,

I will escape the dark".

Tears of the forgotten girl; a collection of short poems

She studies a craft to help others see,

And she plans her resurgence from them,

She has amassed the means to break free,

Emerging from the chasm,

No longer with sorrow and never with hate,

But the weary soul cannot escape with her,

She whispers to her "You will find happiness".

Tears fall for this bequeath.

No longer a reason for her to endure,

The long years of sadness now behind her,

She runs far away never to return,

Freeing their paper claim.

A violent storm disturbs the girl's dream,

Startled by a deafening noise, she turns,

Toward the terrible events that unfold,

As the Bowman takes aim…

Tears of the forgotten girl; a collection of short poems

~

Tears of the forgotten girl; a collection of short poems

Chronology and location of key events

Tears of the forgotten girl; a collection of short poems

Date	Poem	Location
22 December 1999	*The intervention*	Cambridge
7 March 2000	*Mortal touch*	London
1 February 2001	*Sealed in the rain*	Gabriel's Wharf (London)
1 January 2002	*Beauty unrivalled*	Bernese Oberland (Switzerland)
25 December 2003	*Luminous intensity*	Andaman Sea (Malaysia)
21 April 2004	*The rider ascends*	N/A
11 September 2005	*Embraced by a father*	Cambridge
22 June 2006	*A new champion*	London
14 October 2007	*A bold advance*	Schiphol Airport (Amsterdam)
18 December 2008	*Force of will*	Cambridge
20 July 2009	*Defiant one*	Oxford
31 October 2010	*The rider falters*	N/A
27 November 2011	*A final intervention*	Oxford
N/A	*The forgotten girl*	London

Tears of the forgotten girl; a collection of short poems

~

Tears of the forgotten girl; a collection of short poems

Appendices: Poems by Nita Mahalingham

Tears of the forgotten girl; a collection of short poems

Appendix I: The bond between a parent and a child

Tears of the forgotten girl; a collection of short poems

The bond between a parent and a child lasts a lifetime…

The bond between a parent and a child is a special one

It remains unchanged by time or distance.

It is the purest love,

Unconditional and true.

It is an understanding of any situation

And forgiving of any mistake…

The bond between a parent and a child

Creates a support that is constant while everything changes.

It is a friendship based on mutual love, respect,

And genuine liking of each other as a person.

It is knowing that no matter where you go or who you are,

There is someone who truly loves you

And is always there to support and console you.

When a situation seems impossible,

You make it through together by holding onto one another.

Tears of the forgotten girl; a collection of short poems

The bond between a parent and a child

Is strong enough to withstand harsh words and feelings,

For it is smart enough to always see the love beyond the words.

It is brave enough to speak the truth,

Even when lies would be easier.

It is always there

Anytime, anywhere

Whenever it is needed.

It is a gift held in the heart

And in the soul,

And it cannot be taken away or exchanged for another.

To possess this love is a treasure

That makes life more valuable.

Tears of the forgotten girl; a collection of short poems

~

Tears of the forgotten girl; a collection of short poems

Appendix II: On the birth of our first child

Tears of the forgotten girl; a collection of short poems

On the birth of our first child,

I wanted to say more than just "I love you"

Sometimes it's not enough just to say "I love you"

I feel the need to express more,

Because there is so much more to us…

Sometimes I need to tell you

You're the love that I live for,

You're my dream made into reality.

Yours are the arms that hold me close,

And it is your smile that brings that ray of sunshine

To even the darkest of days.

You are the one who tells me to keep believing in myself,

In you, and in us.

You have become a part of me I could never live without,

And as long as I'm living,

I'll be here for you and our new family,

Tears of the forgotten girl; a collection of short poems

And I'll do anything for us.

This is a special time in our lives

Because we are sharing this miracle of life together,

I love you.

Tears of the forgotten girl; a collection of short poems

~

Tears of the forgotten girl; a collection of short poems

About the author

Tears of the forgotten girl; a collection of short poems

The author was born in the UK in February 1976, the second son of first generation settlers from Sri-Lanka. He was caught up in the 1983 riots in the nation's capital, Columbo whilst visiting relatives and forced to hide from murderous thugs (armed with petrol cans, torches and clubs). He spent two nights sheltering with his elder brother and mother in a basement no more than 10 feet across shared with other innocents trying to escape a violent death at the hands of a bloodthirsty mob. This introduced him to the atrocities of civil war at a young age and framed his views on suffering and hardship.

He was educated in the UK and works in Central London; He is happily married to Nita and they have three children.

This is his only poetical work to date.

May 2012

Tears of the forgotten girl; a collection of short poems

~

Tears of the forgotten girl; a collection of short poems

End notes

Tears of the forgotten girl; a collection of short poems

i. The Mahabharatha is an epic Hindu text detailing the impact of a war between the Pandavas and the Kauravas (who are essentially cousins) fighting over the Kingdom of Hastinapura in ancient India. Many of the central characters are demi-gods with immense power and the text provides a treatment of the concept of dharma – natural law and balance.

ii. Ksatriya is one of the four castes/social orders of ancient India (Brahmin - saint, Ksatriya – military/royal, Vaisya - merchant, Sudra -labourer).

iii. The Bhagavad Gita is a 700 verse poem contained within the Mahabharata considering the path to self-realisation. The eminent scholar Henry David Thoreau once commented: "in the morning I bathe my intellect in the stupendous and cosmogonal philosophy of the Bhagavad Gita, in comparison with which our modern world and its literature seem puny and trivial".

iv. The Oxford English Dictionary defines "Cimmerian" as dark, gloomy or devoid of light (Greek mythological derivation).

v. The author refers to "The Bowman" in the text to represent the Hindu God, Lord Shiva; Lord Shiva is the destroyer and the harbinger of death and believed to determine the fate of all mankind. The Hindu God of Death (Lord Yama) is subservient to Lord Shiva and there are many anecdotes from Hindu mythology whereby those on their death bed will appeal to Lord Shiva for clemency to circumvent Lord Yama. Lord Shiva is symbolised by a crescent moon.

vi. Suus angelus is Latin for "her angel".

vii. "The path of Kings" is a reference to Kings Road in London where the author first met the forgotten girl.

viii. The references to murky waters are to the River Thames; as described in the text, this river froze in 1900, some 100 years before the events described.

ix. The events being described took place in the year 2000 – the offering "carved once in a thousand years" refers to a millennium cut ring.

x. "The fortress of ice" refers to the Bernese Oberland mountain range in Switzerland.

xi. The events being described take place at Lake Brienz (in Switzerland).

xii. The reference here is to Sri Lanka, the ancestral home of the author. Sri Lanka was called Serendip at the time of the events described.

xiii. This reference is to the Lake of the Pregnant Maiden (Dayang Buntang) in Malaysia which is visited by many every year who believe the water to have spiritual power.

xiv. "Born under the watchful eyes of great twins" refers to the Zodiacal sign of Gemini (May 21st – June 20th).

xv. Karna was a central character from the Mahabharata described above and fought with the Kauravas despite being the brother of the Pandavas. He was characterised by courage and skill in addition to unquestioning loyalty (hence "Karnan adherence").

xvi. "The bane of Ksatriya" refers to Parasurama, a character, also from the Mahabharata, who was characterised by indomitable strength and who annihilated generations of sinful warriors from the Ksatriya caste after his father was murdered by one of said caste. He stands out in Hindu mythology as an individual whose revenge and retribution against those who harmed his family was unequalled.

xvii. ibid - See reference above to Parasurama whose weapon was the axe ("Parasu" in Sanskrit).

Tears of the forgotten girl; a collection of short poems

xviii. Surya is the Hindu Sun God and his "charge with centaur" denotes late November/December when the Sun enters the Zodiac house of Sagittarius.

xix. "Assured of liberation in the Supreme" is a translation from the Bhagavad Gita to indicate that the soul will find peace in the afterlife.

Tears of the forgotten girl; a collection of short poems

Printed and bound by Lulu Publishing in the United States

May 2012

Tears of the forgotten girl; a collection of short poems

Tears of the forgotten girl; a collection of short poems

Tears of the forgotten girl; a collection of short poems

Tears of the forgotten girl; a collection of short poems

Tears of the forgotten girl; a collection of short poems

Tears of the forgotten girl; a collection of short poems

Tears of the forgotten girl; a collection of short poems

Tears of the forgotten girl; a collection of short poems

Tears of the forgotten girl; a collection of short poems

Tears of the forgotten girl; a collection of short poems

Tears of the forgotten girl; a collection of short poems

Tears of the forgotten girl; a collection of short poems

May 2012

Tears of the forgotten girl; a collection of short poems

.

Tears of the forgotten girl; a collection of short poems

Tears of the forgotten girl; a collection of short poems

Tears of the forgotten girl; a collection of short poems

Tears of the forgotten girl; a collection of short poems

Tears of the forgotten girl; a collection of short poems

Tears of the forgotten girl; a collection of short poems

May 2012

Tears of the forgotten girl; a collection of short poems

_____

www.ingramcontent.com/pod-product-compliance
Lightning Source LLC
Chambersburg PA
CBHW070833100426
42813CB00003B/596